My Notebook

Giant-Sized Notebook

My Journal

Giant-Sized Notebook

Jumbo Notebook/Journal with 600 Lined & Numbered Pages: Milky Way Galaxy Cover Design Composition Notebook 8.5 x 11 - 300 Sheets

Copyright © 2018 Othen Donald Dale Cummings, My Journal

All rights reserved.

ISBN-13: 978-1725587458
ISBN: 1725587459

This

NOTEBOOK

Belongs To:

_____

My Notebook

My Journal

My Notebook

My Journal

My Notebook

My Journal

My Notebook

My Journal

My Notebook

My Journal

My Notebook

My Journal

My Notebook

My Journal

My Notebook

My Journal

My Notebook

My Journal

My Notebook

My Journal

My Notebook

My Journal

My Notebook

My Journal

My Notebook

My Journal

My Notebook

My Journal

My Notebook

My Journal

My Notebook

My Journal

My Notebook

My Journal

My Notebook

My Journal

My Notebook

My Journal

My Notebook

My Journal

My Notebook

My Journal

My Notebook

My Journal

My Notebook

My Journal

My Notebook

My Journal

My Notebook

My Journal

My Notebook

My Journal

My Notebook

My Journal

My Notebook

My Journal

My Notebook

My Journal

My Notebook

My Journal

My Notebook

My Journal

My Notebook

My Journal

My Notebook

My Journal

My Notebook

My Journal

My Notebook

My Journal

My Notebook

My Journal

My Notebook

My Journal

My Notebook

My Journal

My Notebook

My Journal

My Notebook

My Journal

My Notebook

My Journal

My Notebook

My Journal

My Notebook

My Journal

My Notebook

My Journal

My Notebook

My Journal

My Notebook

My Journal

My Notebook

My Journal

My Notebook

My Journal

My Notebook

My Journal

My Notebook

My Journal

My Notebook

My Journal

My Notebook

My Journal

My Notebook

My Journal

My Notebook

My Journal

My Notebook

My Journal

My Notebook

My Journal

My Notebook

My Journal

My Notebook

My Journal

My Notebook

My Journal

My Notebook

My Journal

My Notebook

My Journal

My Notebook

My Journal

My Notebook

My Journal

My Notebook

My Journal

My Notebook

My Journal

My Notebook

My Journal

My Notebook

My Journal

My Notebook

My Journal

My Notebook

My Journal

My Notebook

My Journal

My Notebook

My Journal

My Notebook

My Journal

My Notebook

My Journal

My Notebook

My Journal

My Notebook

My Journal

My Notebook

My Journal

My Notebook

My Journal

My Notebook

My Journal

My Notebook

My Journal

My Notebook

My Journal

My Notebook

My Journal

My Notebook

My Journal

My Notebook

My Journal

My Notebook

My Journal

My Notebook

My Journal

My Notebook

My Journal

My Notebook

My Journal

ND# My Notebook

My Journal

My Notebook

My Journal

My Notebook

My Journal

My Notebook

My Journal

My Notebook

My Journal

My Notebook

My Journal

My Notebook

My Journal

My Notebook

My Journal

My Notebook

My Journal

My Notebook

My Journal

My Notebook

My Journal

My Notebook

My Journal

My Notebook

My Journal

My Notebook

My Journal

My Notebook

My Journal

My Notebook

My Journal

My Notebook

My Journal

My Notebook

My Journal

My Notebook

My Journal

My Notebook

My Journal

My Notebook

My Journal

My Notebook

My Journal

My Notebook

My Journal

My Notebook

My Journal

My Notebook

My Journal

My Notebook

My Journal

My Notebook

My Journal

My Notebook

My Journal

My Notebook

My Journal

My Notebook

My Journal

My Notebook

My Journal

My Notebook

My Journal

My Notebook

My Journal

My Notebook

My Journal

My Notebook

My Journal

My Notebook

My Journal

My Notebook

My Journal

My Notebook

My Journal

My Notebook

My Journal

My Notebook

My Journal

My Notebook

My Journal

My Notebook

My Journal

My Notebook

My Journal

My Notebook

My Journal

My Notebook

My Journal

My Notebook

My Journal

My Notebook

My Journal

My Notebook

My Journal

My Notebook

My Journal

My Notebook

My Journal

My Notebook

My Journal

My Notebook

My Journal

My Notebook

My Journal

My Notebook

My Journal

My Notebook

My Journal

My Notebook

My Journal

My Notebook

My Journal

My Notebook

My Journal

My Notebook

My Journal

My Notebook

My Journal

My Notebook

My Journal

My Notebook

My Journal

My Notebook

My Journal

My Notebook

My Journal

My Notebook

My Journal

My Notebook

My Journal

My Notebook

My Journal

My Notebook

My Journal

My Notebook

My Journal

My Notebook

My Journal

My Notebook

My Journal

My Notebook

My Journal

My Notebook

My Journal

My Notebook

My Journal

My Notebook

My Journal

My Notebook

My Journal

My Notebook

My Journal

My Notebook

My Journal

My Notebook

My Journal

My Notebook

My Journal

My Notebook

My Journal

My Notebook

My Journal

My Notebook

My Journal

My Notebook

My Journal

My Notebook

My Journal

My Notebook

My Journal

My Notebook

My Journal

My Notebook

My Journal

My Notebook

My Journal

My Notebook

My Journal

My Notebook

My Journal

My Notebook

My Journal

My Notebook

My Journal

My Notebook

My Journal

My Notebook

My Journal

My Notebook

My Journal

My Notebook

My Journal

My Notebook

My Journal

My Notebook

My Journal

My Notebook

My Journal

My Notebook

My Journal

My Notebook

My Journal

My Notebook

My Journal

My Notebook

My Journal

My Notebook

My Journal

My Notebook

My Journal

My Notebook

My Journal

My Notebook

My Journal

My Notebook

My Journal

My Notebook

My Journal

My Notebook

My Journal

My Notebook

My Journal

My Notebook

My Journal

My Notebook

My Journal

My Notebook

My Journal

My Notebook

My Journal

My Notebook

My Journal

My Notebook

My Journal

My Notebook

My Journal

My Notebook

My Journal

My Notebook

My Journal

My Notebook

My Journal

My Notebook

My Journal

My Notebook

My Journal

My Notebook

My Journal

My Notebook

My Journal

My Notebook

My Journal

My Notebook

My Journal

My Notebook

My Journal

My Notebook

My Journal

My Notebook

My Journal

My Notebook

My Journal

My Notebook

My Journal

My Notebook

My Journal

My Notebook

My Journal

My Notebook

My Journal

My Notebook

My Journal

My Notebook

My Journal

My Notebook

My Journal

My Notebook

My Journal

My Notebook

My Journal

My Notebook

My Journal

My Notebook

My Journal

My Notebook

My Journal

My Notebook

My Journal

My Notebook

My Journal

My Notebook

My Journal

My Notebook

My Journal

My Notebook

My Journal

My Notebook

My Journal

My Notebook

My Journal

My Notebook

My Journal

My Notebook

My Journal

My Notebook

My Journal

My Notebook

My Journal

My Notebook

My Journal

My Notebook

My Journal

My Notebook

My Journal

My Notebook

My Journal

My Notebook

My Journal

My Notebook

My Journal

My Notebook

My Journal

My Notebook

My Journal

My Notebook

My Journal

My Notebook

My Journal

My Notebook

My Journal

My Notebook

My Journal

My Notebook

My Journal

My Notebook

My Journal

My Notebook

My Journal

My Notebook

My Journal

My Notebook

My Journal

My Notebook

My Journal

My Notebook

My Journal

My Notebook

My Journal

My Notebook

My Journal

My Notebook

My Journal

My Notebook

My Journal

My Notebook

My Journal

My Notebook

My Journal

My Notebook

My Journal

My Notebook

My Journal

My Notebook

My Journal

My Notebook

My Journal

My Notebook

My Journal

My Notebook

My Journal

My Notebook

My Journal

My Notebook

My Journal

My Notebook

My Journal

My Notebook

My Journal

My Notebook

My Journal

My Notebook

My Journal

My Notebook

My Journal

My Notebook

My Journal

My Notebook

My Journal

My Notebook

My Journal

My Notebook

My Journal

My Notebook

My Journal

My Notebook

My Journal

My Notebook

My Journal

My Notebook

My Journal

My Notebook

My Journal

My Notebook

My Journal

My Notebook

My Journal

My Notebook

My Journal

My Notebook

My Journal

My Notebook

My Journal

My Notebook

My Journal

My Notebook

My Journal

My Notebook

My Journal

My Notebook

My Journal

My Notebook

My Journal

My Notebook

My Journal

My Notebook

Made in the USA
Coppell, TX
08 November 2020